Handbook for Ranking Exotic Plants for Management and Control

Ronald D. Hiebert

National Park Service
Midwest Regional Office
1709 Jackson Street
Omaha, NE 68102

and

James Stubbendieck

Department of Agronomy
University of Nebraska
Lincoln, NE 68583

Natural Resources Report NPS/NRMWRO/NRR-93/08

July 1993

U. S. Department of the Interior
National Park Service
Natural Resources Publication Office
Denver, Colorado

Contents

Figures

Tables

Introduction

Exotic, alien, introduced, nonindigenous, and nonnative are all synonyms for species that humans intentionally or unintentionally introduced into an area outside of a species' natural range. The National Park Service (NPS) defines exotic species as those occurring in a given place as a result of direct or indirect, deliberate, or accidental actions of humans. Thus, species native to the North American continent if outside their normal range due to the actions of humans are considered exotics by the National Park Service. The reader is directed to the *Natural Resources Management Guideline* (U.S. Department of the Interior, National Park Service 1991, NPS-77) to further clarify the definition.

Most exotic plant species cause minor effects on natural ecosystems. For example, Great Smoky Mountains National Park has approximately 1,500 vascular plant species, 400 of which are exotics -- 10 species are considered to be threatening to park resources. Of the 1,400 vascular plants at Indiana Dunes National Lakeshore, 300 are exotics, 14 of which are considered to be major threats. However, some exotic species can be extremely disruptive, such as disrupting the accurate presentation of a historic scene, damaging historic or archeological resources, interfering with natural processes, and threatening the survival of naturally evolved plant assemblages and individual native species.

Exotic species are often major roadblocks to managing natural resources in parks and other natural areas. Managing exotic plants is an extremely expensive, labor-intensive, and almost always a long-term proposition. Managers must not only be concerned with the level of impact that an exotic can cause but must also consider the impact of removing the species. Removal can often disturb areas that are easily colonized by the same or other exotic species (Westman 1990). The intensity and longevity of a control program are also important factors to consider in managing exotic plants. Therefore, managers must make sound decisions on where to place one's effort.

NPS policies, as they relate to managing natural resources, require that managers implement programs to maintain, restore, and perpetuate fundamental ecological processes as well as individual species and features. Managers are directed to manage not only for individual species but to maintain all the components and processes of naturally evolving park ecosystems (U.S. Department of the Interior, National Park Service 1988). Specific NPS policy on exotic species directs park managers to give high priority to controlling and managing exotic species that have substantial impacts on park resources and that are believed to be easily managed. High priority should also be given to managing and monitoring exotic plant species that presently may not cause major impacts to park resources but have life history characteristics associated with colonizing or weedy species (Baker 1965) or are known to cause major impacts in other natural areas. Low priority should be given to species that cause little impact, are virtually impossible to control, or both.

A ranking system has been developed for resource managers to sort exotic plants within a park according to the species level of impact and its innate ability to become a pest. This information can then be weighed against the perceived feasibility or ease of control. The Exotic Species Ranking System is designed to first separate the innocuous species from the disruptive species. The separation allows researchers to then concentrate further efforts on species in the disruptive category. The system is also designed to identify those species that are not presently a serious threat but have the potential to become a threat and, thus, should be monitored closely. Finally, the system asks the park manager and the ecologist to consider the cost of delaying any action.

This handbook describes the rationale of the ranking system and its components and how to adapt the system to different situations and different areas of the country. The handbook also describes the information that is needed to apply the system, what the user should know, and how to use the system. Examples of products are given, along with suggestions of their application to management.

An Exotic Plant Ranking System

Why Use an Analytical Approach?

Several sound reasons exist for using an analytical approach as the basis of prioritizing exotic species. One of the basic reasons for using a decision analysis process is to get scientists involved in the decision-making process. Using a consistent and logical decision-making process prevents a biologist from compromising scientific excellence by becoming involved in environmental decisions based on incomplete information. Selecting an action alternative is similar to selecting a hypothesis. The action becomes an experimental manipulation to test the validity of the "hypothesis." A decision analysis process not only adds validity to a decision, but this process often demonstrates that inaction due to lack of complete information can have serious consequences (Maguire 1991).

If an analytical approach was not employed, decisions would most likely be based on the opinion of an individual or a group of individuals or decisions would be based on precedent. Granted, many field ecologists have a good idea of which exotic species are impacting natural ecosystem processes or impacting species composition. However, decisions based on judgment alone are rarely based on defined criteria, do not usually document the reasoning process, and give no assurance that the full array of significant factors were considered. Such decisions may suffer from personal biases and political whims. Decisions are hard to defend if challenged, and proposals for funding are hard to justify. Decisions based on precedent may be easier to defend but are not responsive to the variation in exotic species or natural system interactions over space and time. Thus, priorities set for managing exotic species based on precedent may not reflect current ecological and economic realities.

On the other hand, consistently using an analytical tool, such as the Exotic Species Ranking System, can ensure that ecological knowledge is applied to the decision process and can remedy some of the problems associated with decisions based on judgment and precedent alone. An analytical framework encourages researchers to consider the full range of factors and consequences of their decisions. An analytical framework documents the procedures and the reasons for the decisions made, thus reducing the risk aversion characteristic of park managers. Decisions are defendable. Solid justification for program authorization and funding is at hand.

Origin

An earlier version of the system presented here was developed by Ron Hiebert. The system was modeled after a ranking system that was developed at Point Reyes National Seashore (Self 1986). The purpose of this system was to rank the effects of exotic species on the natural recovery of former residential sites at Indiana Dunes National Lakeshore. Hiebert (1990) observed that some exotic species were found only in severely and recently disturbed areas and seemed to have little effect on the succession process. Other exotic species were persistent but did not reproduce or spread, while others were persistent and had high rates of reproduction. Populations of some exotics were expanding within disturbed areas, while others were observed to invade surrounding undisturbed sites. Some of the most invasive and disruptive species were those with life history characteristics (high seed output, long-distance dispersal adaptations, ability to reproduce vegetatively) consistent with those related to weediness (Baker 1965). The present system was developed to support general NPS and park-specific policy, giving high priority to species causing major impacts (and are easily controlled) and giving low priority to species causing little impact (and extremely difficult to control).

Also, the system is designed to identify species that are currently rare and causing little impact but have a high potential to become a problem in the future.

The ranking system presented in this handbook has since been applied to ranking the exotic plants of Indiana Dunes (Klick et al. 1989) and six small national park system areas dominated by prairies and savannahs (Stubbendieck et al. 1992). As part of the latter, 14 plant ecologists reviewed the system. The system was modified to rank exotic plants in Olympic National Park (Olson et al. 1991) and was modified and used to rank both exotic plants and animals in the state of Minnesota (Minnesota Department of Natural Resources 1991). The system has been revised based on the above experiences and recommendations of users and expert reviewers.

Rationale For Use

The ranking system provides an ecologist or resource management specialist with a tool to sort exotic plant species based on their present level of impact and their innate ability to become a pest. Based on conscientious consideration of all the factors in the system, a person with good taxonomic and ecological skills should be able to separate those species that are innocuous from those that are disruptive or have a high potential to become disruptive. The resulting species rank can then be weighed against the ease or feasibility of control, and the urgency of action or the cost of delay in action can be determined.

For example, purple loosestrife (*Lythrum salicaria*) is ranked as the most disruptive exotic plant at Indiana Dunes National Lakeshore. Extensive efforts to eradicate or control its spread have not been successful. However, due to the significance of the impact, the National Park Service is funding research on its basic biology and on experimental control methods. In contrast, Scotch pine (*Pinus sylvestris*) is found to rarely reproduce and to cause only minor impacts throughout most of the park. Significant impacts are limited to one small prairie opening. Control is relatively simple--saw the pine down. Therefore, the park decided to eradicate Scotch pine from the prairie opening and to monitor its status in other park locations.

An example of the urgency ranking as applied is European alder (*Alnus glutinosa*). This species was found at or in close proximity to one razed residential site at Indiana Dunes National Lakeshore. However, the species had spread into a large, dense clone of thousands of ramets in just six years and was also reproducing sexually. The species was reported to be highly invasive and to cause major impacts in other natural areas. Therefore, the National Park Service considered quick action to be prudent.

In summary, the ranking system encourages resource managers to logically apply criteria that address the present impact of a species on ecological processes and structure and on other park resources. The ranking system also predicts the potential of a species to become a pest in the future. Normally, applying the system will greatly reduce the list of exotic species with which a park manager needs to be concerned. The decision to take management action against a species determined to be disruptive then can be weighed on the basis of the level of impact, the feasibility of successful control, and the prediction of the cost of delay in action. The information accumulated in the system's application serves as solid documentation to support management's decisions and to justify program funding.

Description

The Exotic Species Ranking System in Table 1 uses numerical ratings, is written in outline format, and is divided into two main sections: I. Significance of Impact and II. Feasibility of Control or Management. Each section is based on a scale of 100 points.

Table 1. Exotic Species Ranking System.

Exotic Species Ranking System Ronald D. Hiebert	
I. Significance of Impact	
A. Current Level of Impact	
1. Distribution relative to disturbance regime	
a. found only within sites disturbed within the last 3 years of sites regularly disturbed	-10
b. found in sites disturbed within the last 10 years	1
c. found in midsuccessional sites disturbed 11-50 years before present (BP)	2
d. found in late-successional sites disturbed 51-100 years BP	5
e. found in high-quality natural areas with no known major disturbance for 100 years	10
2. Abundance	
a. number of populations (stands)	
(1) few; scattered (<5)	1
(2) intermediate number; patchy (6-10)	3
(3) several; widespread and dense (>10)	5
b. areal extent of populations	
(1) <5 ha	1
(2) 5-10 ha	2
(3) 11-50 ha	3
(4) >50 ha	5
3. Effect on natural processes and character	
a. plant species having little or no effect	0
b. delays establishment of native species in disturbed sites up to 10 years	3
c. long-term (more than 10 years) modification or retardation of succession	7
d. invades and modifies existing native communities	10
e. invades and replaces native communities	15
4. Significance of threat to park resources	
a. threat to secondary resources negligible	0
b. threat to areas' secondary (successional) resources	2
c. endangerment to areas' secondary (successional) resources	4
d. threat to areas' primary resources	8
e. endangerment to areas' primary resources	10

Table 1 (cont).

5. Level of visual impact to an ecologist
   a. little or no visual impact on landscape — 0
   b. minor visual impact on natural landscape — 2
   c. significant visual impact on natural landscape — 4
   d. major visual impact on natural landscape — 5

   Total Possible = 50

B. Innate Ability of Species to Become a Pest

1. Ability to complete reproductive cycle in area of concern
   a. not observed to complete reproductive cycle — 0
   b. observed to complete reproductive cycle — 5
2. Mode of reproduction
   a. reproduces almost entirely by vegetative means — 1
   b. reproduces only by seeds — 3
   c. reproduces vegetatively and by seed — 5
3. Vegetative reproduction
   a. no vegetative reproduction — 0
   b. vegetative reproduction rate maintains population — 1
   c. vegetative reproduction rate results in moderate increase in population size — 3
   d. vegetative reproduction rate results in rapid increase in population size — 5
4. Frequency of sexual reproduction for mature plant
   a. almost never reproduces sexually in area — 0
   b. once every five or more years — 1
   c. every other year — 3
   d. one or more times a year — 5
5. Number of seeds per plant
   a. few (0-10) — 1
   b. moderate (11-1,000) — 3
   c. many-seeded (>1,000) — 5
6. Dispersal ability
   a. little potential for long-distance dispersal — 0
   b. great potential for long-distance dispersal — 5
7. Germination requirements
   a. requires open soil and disturbance to germinate — 0
   b. can germinate in vegetated areas but in a narrow range or in special conditions — 3
   c. can germinate in existing vegetation in a wide range of conditions — 5
8. Competitive ability
   a. poor competitor for limiting factors — 0
   b. moderately competitive for limiting factors — 3
   c. highly competitive for limiting factors — 5
9. Known level of impact in natural areas
   a. not known to cause impacts in any other natural area — 0
   b. known to cause impacts in natural areas, but in other habitats and different climate zones — 1
   c. known to cause low impact in natural areas in similar habitats and climate zones — 3
   d. known to cause moderate impact in natural areas in similar habitats and climate zones — 5
   e. known to cause high impact in natural areas in similar habitats and climate zones — 10

   Total Possible = 50

Table 1 (cont).

II. Feasibility of Control or Management
   A. Abundance Within Park
      1. Number of populations (stands)
         a. several; widespread and dense   1
         b. intermediate number; patchy   3
         c. few; scattered   5
      2. Areal extent of populations
         a. > 50 ha   1
         b. 11-50 ha   2
         c. 5-10 ha   3
         d. <5 ha   5
   B. Ease of Control
      1. Seed banks
         a. seeds remain viable in the soil for at least 3 years   0
         b. seeds remain viable in the soil for 2-3 years   5
         c. seeds viable in the soil for 1 year or less   15
      2. Vegetative regeneration
         a. any plant part is a viable propagule   0
         b. sprouts from roots or stumps   5
         c. no resprouting following removal of aboveground growth   10
      3. Level of effort required
         a. repeated chemical or mechanical control measures required   1
         b. one or two chemical or mechanical treatments required   5
         c. can be controlled with one chemical treatment   10
         d. effective control can be achieved with mechanical treatment   15
      4. Abundance and proximity of propagules near park
         a. many sources of propagules near park   0
         b. few sources of propagules near park, but these are readily dispersed   5
         c. few sources of propagules near park, but these are not readily dispersed   10
         d. no sources of propagules are in close proximity   15
   C. Side Effects of Chemical/Mechanical Control Measures
      1. control measures will cause major impacts to community   0
      2. control measures will cause moderate impacts to community   5
      3. control measures will have little or no impact on community   15
   D. Effectiveness of Community Management
      1. the following options are not effective   0
      2. cultural techniques (burning, flooding) can be used to control target species   5
      3. routine management of community or restoration or preservation practices (e.g., prescribed burning, flooding, controlled disturbance) effectively controls target species   10
   E. Biological Control
      1. biological control not feasible (not practical, possible, or probable)   0
      2. potential may exist for biological control   5
      3. biological control feasible   10

                                             Total Possible = 100

Urgency
1. Delay in action will result in large increase in effort required for successful control.   High
2. Delay in action will result in moderate increase in effort required for successful control.   Medium
3. Delay in action will result in little increase in effort required for successful control.   Low

I. Significance of Impact is further divided into A. Current Level of Impact and B. Innate Ability of Species to Become a Pest. Stubbendieck et al. (1992) considered a species with a combined score of over 50 points for significance of impact to be seriously disruptive and needing appropriate attention. Species receiving high scores for feasibility of control will be easier to control than those receiving lower scores. A step-by-step description of the system follows.

I. Significance of Impact

A. Current Level of Impact: This section concentrates on ranking the species based on the present degree and extent of impact caused by the exotic species. Element 1 addresses where the species is found along a disturbance regime. If the species is found in only sites that are recently or frequently disturbed, the species is not considered a serious threat. If the species is found in mature undisturbed natural communities, the species is considered a serious threat. Element 2 addresses how many populations (stands) are found in the park and the size of the populations. Element 3 rates a species based on its effects on the ecological processes and structure of native communities. Element 4 addresses which park resources are threatened. Finally, element 5 addresses the visual impact as seen by an ecologist.

B. Innate Ability of Species to Become a Pest: This section ranks a species based on the life history traits that preadapt it to become a problem and its known impacts in other areas. Important life history characteristics include potential rate of increase, adaptations for long-distance dispersal, and the breadth of habitats in which the species can colonize and thrive. Element 1 is essentially a screening device. If the species cannot reproduce in the area, the species most likely will not pose much of a threat. Likely species that will not reproduce in an area are horticultural species transferred from areas with different environmental conditions. Element 2 addresses how a species reproduces. The assumption is that vegetative reproduction allows an adapted ecotype to be maintained, resulting in local spread. Sexual reproduction allows for the maintenance of genetic variation and propagules for long-distance dispersal and the possibility of forming highly adapted gene combinations. If the species can reproduce both vegetatively and sexually, that species has the best of both worlds.

Elements 3, 4, and 5 address the factors that determine the intrinsic rate of increase of a species--how many seeds are produced how often. Element 6 deals with the species ability to disperse. This factor can usually be rated based on the presence or absence of special adaptations for seed or fruit dispersal, such as wings and pappi for wind dispersal, bladders for water dispersal, or bristles for animal dispersal. Element 7 asks if the species needs bare soil (disturbed) to germinate or if the species can germinate in a relatively closed (undisturbed) community. Element 8 looks at what the species can do once the species has colonized an area. Is the species able to outcompete native species for light, water, etc.? Finally, scientists should not ignore what the effects of the species have been in other natural areas.

II. Feasibility of Control or Management

Less is known about the feasibility of managing exotic plants in natural areas than what impacts they have on the natural systems. Most research efforts in controlling plants have been in agriculture where the goal is to control all but one species while not harming the single-crop species. In natural areas, the goal is to control one or a few species while not harming diverse assemblages of native species. However, many factors will affect the funds and effort required for control and the probability of success.

A. Abundance Within Park: No explanation is needed here. The larger the populations and the larger the number of populations, the larger the funds and effort required to manage the species.

B. Ease of Control: This section not only deals with life history characteristics that impact the level of effort that will be needed to control the species, but also the probability of success if unlimited funds and personnel are used. Element 1 addresses the seed bank which directly influences the needed duration of a control program. Information on the longevity of viable seeds in soil is not available for many species, therefore making this element hard to score. However, a best estimate should be made based on the information that is available. Element 2 addresses the vegetative reproduction of the species, which influences the number and kinds of treatments required to control the species, whether the underground parts of the plant must be removed, and also dictates the protocol for disposal of plant material. Element 3 not only addresses the level of effort required, but also the kind(s) of control measures required. Element 3 follows the preferred steps of the NPS Integrated Pest Management Program in that mechanical treatment is preferred over chemical treatment. Element 4 deals with the presence or absence of propagules adjacent to the park and the probability of propagules being dispersed into the park. Consideration should be given to the park's ability to control the species outside its boundaries through cooperative control programs.

C. Side Effects of Chemical/Mechanical Control Measures: As stated earlier, researchers must consider what effects eradication or control measures will have on the system being restored or preserved. Will the treatment open up areas for the same species to recolonize or be invaded by other equally or more impacting exotics? In some cases, the lesser of two unsatisfactory options may be not taking any action.

D. Effectiveness of Community Management: Controlling exotic species through sound management of the system based on ecological study is by far the preferred control method. In some cases, controlling trampling by visitors, restoring historical fire regimes, or restoring shoreline processes or natural hydrological regimes will shift the competitive edge to the desired native species.

E. Biological Control: Biological control is ecologically feasible for many exotic species. However, due to the high costs to develop well-tested biological control agents, it is only economically feasible for exotic species causing major impacts over a broad geographical area and normally only if the species are causing an economic impact as well as an ecological impact. Similarly, biological control is not feasible if the species to be controlled has some economic value. Abundance of closely related native species in the area where the exotic is to be controlled also lowers the feasibility because of possible negative side effects. The responsibility of conducting long-term studies involved with selecting and screening possible control agents lies with the U.S. Department of Agriculture.

Urgency: After the species are ranked according to their level of impact and feasibility of control or management, the exotic species that demands the most attention should be addressed first. The cost of delaying an action either financially or in impact to the natural resources of the park is a good criterion to use in making this often difficult decision.

How to Use the System

Work will be conducted both in the field and in the library. Individuals using the Exotic Species Ranking System must have training in biology because the system requires interpreting specific biological information on each species in the field as well as in the literature. A working knowledge of plant taxonomy is required to properly identify species in the field. Identification may be difficult for the less trained because some of the exotic species are members of genera containing native species as well, and proper separation may be made on relatively fine differences between plants.

The first step in using the Exotic Species Ranking System is to inventory the exotic plant species. Names of plant species should be assembled from (1) species lists and research reports for the park, (2) the catalog of specimens from the park herbarium, and (3) a preliminary field survey of the vegetation. Each species on the completed list should be checked in references, especially the flora for the area, to determine if a species is native or exotic.

The second step is to conduct an intensive survey of the park. The survey should include the location and extent of populations of each exotic species. The information obtained in this survey will be used to complete Current Level of Impact (I.A.), a portion of *Innate Ability of Species to Become a Pest* (I.B.), and Abundance within Park (II.A.) Usually, two surveys are required. One survey should be conducted in late spring when most cool-season species are flowering, and the second should be conducted in late summer to correspond with flowering of warm-season species. The extent and number of populations should be drawn on a map during the survey. The map will be important for managers to locate exotic species for continued monitoring and future control.

The third step is a comprehensive search of the literature for information on the ecology, biology, and control methods for each exotic species. Information from this part of the process will be used for a portion of Innate Ability of Species to Become a Pest (I.B.) and the majority of II. Feasibility of Control or Management. Computer data bases in most libraries simplify the search procedure. Key words for the search should include the scientific and common names for each species. Not all of the articles will be applicable, but the computer-generated titles and abstracts generally will indicate whether the complete article should be located. The most commonly used journals are listed in Appendix A. Making photocopies of the article for both the ranking process and to place in the files for future reference may be helpful. Unfortunately, the amount of information in the literature varies considerably with the species. For example, articles on common exotic species such as Kentucky bluegrass (*Poa pratensis*) are abundant. Many of the articles are related to turf and turf grass management and have essentially no value for the ranking process. Considerable time is required to separate articles with useful information from the available literature. On the other hand, the literature contains few articles on less abundant exotic species. Occasionally, ranking an individual species may be difficult because not enough information can be located. For example, no reference may be available that addresses the length of time seeds remain viable in the soil. The person ranking the species may then need to investigate seed bank ecology of other species within the genus or make a decision based on seed morphology.

An additional source of information may be the element stewardship abstracts prepared by The Nature Conservancy. These comprehensive abstracts are available for some of the common species.

The next step of the process is to complete the Exotic Species Ranking System Data Summary Form (see Appendix B for a blank form) for each species by bringing together all of the information that has been gathered in the previous three steps. The person conducting the ranking should read each step of the Exotic Species Ranking System outline in Table 1 and, based on information gathered, select the appropriate numerical value. That value is placed on the Data Summary Form.

An Example: Pipestone National Monument

Intensive exotic species surveys at Pipestone National Monument in Minnesota were conducted during 1989-91. Over 70 exotic species were located and ranked using the Exotic Species Ranking System (Table 2); 11 species were ranked as being highly disruptive (a total of 50 or more points for I. Significance of Impact). These results show that a relatively low proportion of the exotic species will be highly disruptive. None of the highly disruptive species was classified as being easy to control (Figure 1).

Of the 11 highly disruptive exotic species, feasibility of control of quackgrass (*Agropyron repens*) scored the least (16), while feasibility of control of white sweetclover (*Melilotus alba*) scored the greatest (48). Based on knowledge of the individual exotic species, control of only Canada thistle (*Cirsium arvense*) was considered to be urgent.

Canada Thistle

A Data Summary Form for Canada thistle at Pipestone National Monument is presented in Table 3. The data summary in Table 3 may be compared to the outline of the Exotic Species Ranking System in Table 1 to see how Canada thistle was evaluated for each step.

Species Abstract

An additional product that may be obtained from the Exotic Species Ranking System is an abstract for each important species. Generally, important species are those ranked as highly disruptive (a total of 50 or more points for I. Significance of Impact). An outline of the format for a species abstract may be found in Table 4. An example of a species abstract prepared for Canada thistle is in Appendix C.

Table 2. Ranking of exotic plant species (arranged alphabetically)at Pipestone National Monument.

| Species | Significance of Impact | | | | |
	Current Level of Impact	Innate Ability to Become a Pest	Total	Feasibility of Control	Urgency
Agropyron cristatum	-8	27	19	56	Low
Agropyron repens	28	36	64	16	Medium
Agrostis stolonifera	7	25	32	41	Low
Asparagus officinalis	4	25	29	65	Low
Brassica kaber	-8	16	8	65	Low
Bromus inermis	42	43	85	18	Medium
Bromus japonicus	18	20	38	51	Low
Bromus tectorum	17	20	37	38	Low
Campanula rapunculoides	6	26	32	46	Low
Capsella bursa-pastoris	-2	17	15	37	Low
Carduus nutans	19	34	53	31	Medium
Chenopodium album	-5	18	13	56	Low
Cirsium arvense	19	40	59	17	High
Cornilla varia	12	32	44	34	Medium
Dianthus armeria	4	16	20	60	Low
Digitaria sanguinalis	13	24	37	36	Medium
Eleagnus angustifolia	17	30	47	30	Medium
Eragrostis cilianensis	-8	16	8	50	Low
Euphorbia esula	24	48	72	31	High
Hesperis matronalis	-4	19	15	63	Low
Kochia scoparia	-8	31	23	55	Low
Lactuca serriola	-4	17	13	49	Low
Lappula echinata	7	32	39	50	Low
Lappula redowskii	6	30	36	50	Low
Leonurus cardiacea	9	19	28	43	Low
Lepidium campestre	13	20	33	33	Low
Linaria vulgaris	18	29	47	41	Medium
Lithospermum arvense	4	23	27	65	Low
Lolium perenne	-8	19	11	50	Low
Lonicera tatarica	33	39	72	25	Medium
Matricaria matricariodes	-8	17	9	65	Low
Medicago lupulina	-5	24	19	41	Low
Medicago sativa	10	34	44	34	Low
Melilotus alba	17	34	51	48	Medium
Melilotus officianilis	14	34	48	42	Medium
Nepeta cataria	9	21	30	46	Low
Philadelphus coronarius	9	22	31	45	Low
Phleum pratense	10	30	40	36	Low

Table 2 (cont).

| Species | Significance of Impact | | | | |
	Current Level of Impact	Innate Ability to Become a Pest	Total	Feasibility of Control	Urgency
Plantago major	-8	24	16	30	Low
Poa compressa	33	34	67	21	Medium
Poa palustris	18	20	38	51	Low
Poa pratensis	38	43	81	23	Medium
Polygonum achoreum	-8	22	14	60	Low
Polygonum aviculare	-4	22	18	46	Low
Polygonum hydropiper	3	30	33	30	Low
Polygonum persicaria	13	21	34	45	Low
Populus nigra	6	30	36	45	Low
Portulaca oleracea	10	24	34	31	Low
Potentilla fruticosa	6	25	31	60	Low
Potentilla recta	18	22	40	31	Low
Ranunculus testiculatus	-8	21	13	75	Low
Rhamnus cathartica	45	44	89	18	Medium
Rumex crispus	-6	27	21	35	Low
Salsola iberica	-6	31	25	75	Low
Setaria faberi	-8	26	18	55	Low
Setaria glauca	-8	29	21	55	Low
Setaria viridis	-2	26	24	38	Low
Silene cserei	-8	16	8	60	Low
Silene pratensis	-8	19	11	60	Low
Sisymbrium altissimum	-8	21	13	60	Low
Solanum dulcamara	-1	22	21	50	Low
Sonchus arvensis	20	39	59	22	Medium
Taraxacum officinale	-4	33	29	34	Low
Thalspi arvense	-8	18	10	55	Low
Tragopogon dubius	7	26	33	31	Low
Trifolium hybridum	-8	25	13	50	Low
Trifolium pratense	18	23	41	36	Low
Trifolium repens	11	29	40	36	Low
Ulmus pumila	18	29	47	36	Low
Verbascum thapsus	15	22	37	36	Medium
Veronica arvensis	6	19	25	55	Low

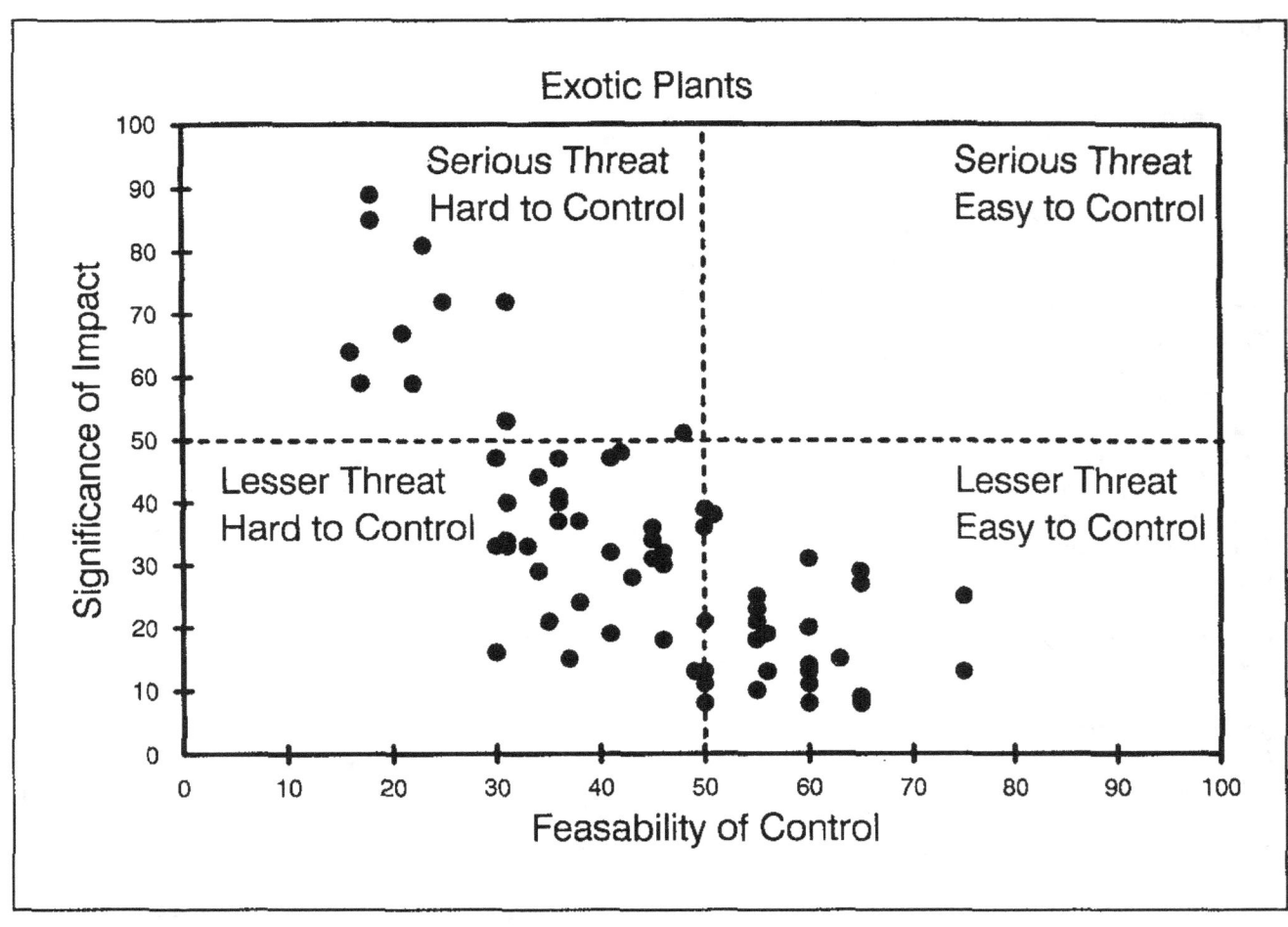

Figure 1. Plot of level of impact vs. feasibility of control for exotic plant species at Pipestone National Monument, Minnesota.

Adaptability

The system presented in this handbook was designed to rank exotic plants in parks and natural areas in the midwestern states with medium-to-high productivity and fairly rapid successional rates. However, the system is designed to be adaptable for different biogeographical areas or groups of organisms, or to be applied at various scales. To adapt the system to different biogeographical areas, the time scale for disturbance regimes can be modified as appropriate. The system was adapted to rank plants and animals at a statewide scale by the state of Minnesota. This ranking was done by the Minnesota Department of Natural Resources. The Minnesota task force applied the system to plants and animals, including birds, mammals, fish, reptiles, amphibians, insects, mollusks, and crustaceans. Rather than use the methods presented here for a single park or natural area, the task force applied them on a statewide basis using averages per county for the abundances ratings.

Table 3. Completed Exotic Species Ranking Summary Form for Canada thistle (*Cirsium arvense*) at Pipestone National Monument.

Exotic Species Ranking System
Data Summary Form

Park: <u>Pipestone National Monument</u>   Species: <u>*Cirsium arvense*</u>

Significance of Impact:

    Current Level of Impact (50)   <u>19</u>

    Innate Ability to Become a Pest (50)   <u>40</u>   Total (100) <u>59</u>

Feasibility of Control: Total (100) <u>17</u>

Urgency: <u>high</u>

I. Significance of Impact:

  A. Current Level of Impact

      1. Distribution relative to disturbance regime (-10, 1, 2, 5, 10)   <u>2</u>
      2. Abundance
         a. number of populations (1, 3, 5)   <u>3</u>
         b. areal extent of populations (1, 2, 3, 5)   <u>1</u>
      3. Effect on natural processes and character (0, 3, 7, 10, 15)   <u>7</u>
      4. Significance of threat to park resources (0, 2, 4, 8, 10)   <u>4</u>
      5. Level of visual impact to an ecologist (0, 2, 4, 5)   <u>2</u>
                             Total (50 possible) <u>19</u>

  B. Innate Ability of Species to Become a Pest

      1. Ability to complete life cycle in area of concern (0, 5)   <u>5</u>
      2. Mode of reproduction (1, 3, 5)   <u>5</u>
      3. Vegetative reproduction (0, 1, 3, 5)   <u>5</u>
      4. Frequency of sexual reproduction (0, 1, 3, 5)   <u>5</u>
      5. Number of seeds per plant (1, 3, 5)   <u>5</u>
      6. Dispersal ability (0, 5)   <u>5</u>
      7. Germination requirements (0, 3, 5)   <u>0</u>
      8. Competitive ability (0, 3, 5)   <u>5</u>
      9. Known level of impact in natural areas (0, 1, 3, 5, 10)   <u>5</u>

                             Total (50 possible) <u>40</u>

                             A + B (100 possible) <u>59</u>

15

Table 3 (cont).

II. Feasibility of Control or Management

  A. Abundance Within Park

      1. Number of populations (1, 3, 5)   3

      2. Areal extent of populations (1, 2, 3, 5)   3

  B. Ease of Control

      1. Seed banks (0, 5, 15)   0

      2. Vegetative regeneration (0, 5, 15)   0

      3. Level of effort required (1, 5, 10, 15)   1

      4. Abundance and proximity of propagules (0, 5, 10, 15)   0

  C. Side Effects of Chemical/Mechanical Control (0, 5, 15)   5

  D. Effectiveness of Community Management (0, 5, 10)   0

  E. Biological Control (0, 5, 10)   5

                                      Total (100 possible)   17

Urgency: high

Table 4. Outline of a species abstract.

Park (full name and abbreviation)

Scientific Name (with authority)

Synonyms (if any)

Common Name(s)

Urgency Ranking

Overall Ranking

Significance of Impact
    A. Current impact
    B. Ability of species to become a pest

Feasibility of Control or Management

Taxonomic Description:
    A. Life form
    B. Height
    C. Vegetative characteristics
       Stems
       Underground (roots, rhizomes, etc.)
       Leaves
          arrangement
          type
          sheaths and ligules (of grasses)
          size
          margins
          surfaces (pubescence)
          attachment
          petiole
    D. Floral characteristics
       Inflorescence
          type
          size
       Flowers of forbs and woody plants
          type
          size
          bracts
          calyx
          corolla
          color
          anthers and ovary
       Spikelets of grasses
          florets
          glumes
          lemmas
          paleas
          awns

Table 4 (cont).

      E. Fruit characteristics
         Type
         Shape
         Size
         Color
         Attachments for dispersal
      F. Varieties (if any)

Biology and Ecology:
      A. Origin
      B. Habitat
      C. Distribution (current and historical)
      D. Climatic and ecological range
         Soils
         Disturbance
         Temperature
         Precipitation
         Soil moisture
         Light
         Fertility
         Other
      E. Reproduction
         Type (asexual or sexual with flowering period)
         Ecological requirements
         Rate
         Seed production (including number per plant)
         Dispersal
         Longevity in seed bank
      F. Germination

Distribution:
      A. Number in the park
      B. Size of populations
      C. *Location and successional sites*
      D. Relationship to disturbance
      E. Invasion potential
      F. Visual impact

Control:
      A. Considerations
      B. Mechanical
      C. Cultural
      D. Chemical
      E. Biological

References:

Local Control Experts:
      A. Extension weed control specialists
      B. Department of Natural Resources
      C. Other

Applying Results to Management Action

The logical species to give the highest priority are those that seriously threaten natural resources yet appear to be easy to control. The lowest priority should be given to those species that pose little threat and would be difficult to control. An easy way to categorize the ranked exotics is to plot the level of impact against the feasibility of control. Plots for Pipestone National Monument and Wilson's Creek National Battlefield are in Figures 1 and 2. As demonstrated in these two cases, the majority of the species are not considered to be a serious threat to park resources. This pattern is consistent with all surveys done to date. Also of note is that no species fall in the quadrant of serious threat and easy to control. We predict that this scenario will be the norm. Deciding which species or group of species in which areas need to be targeted for control is not easy. However, the resource manager now has only a few species to consider and should be equipped with most of the information available to guide a decision. The information will also aid in developing at least rough cost estimates and needed time commitments for various control scenarios. The resource manager also has the background information to defend a decision. The urgency ranking should also help indicate the resource and financial costs of delay in action.

The resource manager may determine that the most serious threat is uncontrollable on a parkwide basis. Control efforts may need to be restricted to rare communities or to areas where the exotic species threatens an endangered species. Control efforts may be futile within the park without cooperation from neighbors, as ample propagules for reinvasion exist near park boundaries. The only known successful control may require using an herbicide that has possible serious side effects. A decision to divert at least a portion of the effort towards investigating ways to shift the competitive advantage from the exotic to the native species or developing methods for easy and economic control of selected exotics may be appropriate. A decision often will require selecting the lesser of several evils. However, with diligence, by soundly applying information to management decisions, and documenting and communicating successful and unsuccessful control efforts, progress can be made in managing exotic species in natural areas.

Cautions

As with any tool, this system can be misused.

1. This ranking system provides a tool to resource managers and biologists who are knowledgeable of the area and species under investigation. They will benefit by using the system to consistently consider all of the important ecological and managerial elements for all exotic species. The ranking system provides the information in a format that can serve as a solid foundation on which to base an action plan. However, as is the case with most tools, the system can be misused or even be harmful if not used as intended or if not used by a skillful craftsman.

2. Separating the innocuous species from the disruptive species and consistently generating information on exotic species is the purpose of the system. The actual numeric values have little meaning or value.

3. The information provided by using this system to survey and rank exotic species is good for a specific place and time. Ecological systems are highly dynamic, and the distribution abundance and level and type of impact will change over time and space.

Literature Cited

Baker, H.G. 1965. Characteristics and modes of origin of weeds. Pages 147-172 *in* H.G. Baker and G.L. Stebbins, editors. The Genetics of Colonizing Species. Academic Press, New York.

Hiebert, R.D. 1990. An ecological restoration model: application to razed residential sites. Natural Areas Journal 10:181-186.

Klick, K., S. O'Brien, and L. Lobik-Klick. 1989. Exotic plants of Indiana Dunes National Lakeshore: a management review of their extent and implications. Report to the U.S. Department of the Interior, National Park Service. 150 pp. + maps.

Maguire, L.A. 1991. Risk analysis for conservation biologists. Conservation Biology 5:123-125.

Minnesota Department of Natural Resources. 1991. Report and recommendations of the Minnesota Interagency Exotic Species Task Force. 25 pp. + appendices.

Olson, R.W., Jr., E.G. Schreiner, and L. Parker. 1991. Management of exotic plants in Olympic National Park. In-house report. U.S. Department of the Interior, National Park Service.

Self, D.W. 1986. *Exotic plant inventory, rating and management planning for Point Reyes National Seashore.* Pages 85-95 *in* L.K. Thomas, editor. Proceedings of the Conference on Science in the National Parks. U.S. Department of the Interior, National Park Service.

Stubbendieck, J., C.H. Butterfield, and T.R. Flessner. 1992. An assessment of exotic plant species at Pipestone National Monument and Wilson's Creek National Battlefield. U.S. Department of the Interior, National Park Service. Final Report.

U.S. Department of the Interior, National Park Service. 1988. Management Policies.

U.S. Department of the Interior, National Park Service. 1991. Natural Resources Management Guideline, NPS-77.

Westman, W.E. 1990. Park management of exotic plant species: problems and issues. Conservation Biology 4:251-260.

Appendix A
Names of Journals of Commonly Used Sources
of Information for Exotic Species

Journals	Journals
Acta Biotheroretica	Phytopathology
African Journal of Ecology	Plant Disease
Agronomy Journal	Plant Physiology
American Journal of Botany	Quarterly Review of Biology
American Midlands Naturalist	Rangelands
American Naturalist	Restoration and Management
Annual Review of Ecology & Systematics	Notes
Annuals of Botany	SIDA
Biological Conservation	Soil Science
Botanical Gazette	Soviet Journal of Ecology
Bulletin of the Torrey Botanical Club	Vegetatio
Canadian Journal of Botany	Weed Research
Canadian Journal of Plant Science	Weed Science
Conservation Biology	Weed Technology
Crop Science	Weeds
Ecological Modelling	
Ecology	
Environmental Ecology	
Environmental Management	
Grass and Forage Science	
Great Basin Naturalist	
HortScience	
Journal of Agricultural Economics	
Journal of Applied Ecology	
Journal of Arid Environments	
Journal of Biogeography	
Journal of Ecology	
Journal of Economic Entomology	
Journal of Entomological Science	
Journal of Range Management	
Journal of Vegetation Science	
Natural Areas Journal	
New Phytologist	
Oecologia	
Oikos	
Paleobiology	
Physiologia Planatarum	

Appendix B
Exotic Species Ranking System
Data Summary Form

Park: _____   Species: _____

Significance of Impact:

    Current Level of Impact (50)   ____

    Innate Ability to Become a Pest (50)   ____   Total (100) ____

Feasibility of Control: Total (100) ____

Urgency: ____

I. Significance of Impact:

  A. Current Level of Impact

    1. Distribution relative to disturbance regime (-10, 1, 2, 5, 10)   ____
    2. Abundance
      a. number of populations (1, 3, 5)   ____
      b. areal extent of populations (1, 2, 3, 5)   ____
    3. Effect on natural processes and character (0, 3, 7, 10, 15)   ____
    4. Significance of threat to park resources (0, 2, 4, 8, 10)   ____
    5. Level of visual impact to an ecologist (0, 2, 4, 5)   ____
                Total (50 possible)   ____

  B. Innate Ability of Species to Become a Pest

    1. Ability to complete life cycle in area of concern (0, 5)   ____
    2. Mode of reproduction (1, 3, 5)   ____
    3. Vegetative reproduction (0, 1, 3, 5)   ____
    4. Frequency of sexual reproduction (0, 1, 3, 5)   ____
    5. Number of seeds per plant (1, 3, 5)   ____
    6. Dispersal ability (0, 5)   ____
    7. Germination requirements (0, 3, 5)   ____
    8. Competitive ability (0, 3, 5)   ____
    9. Known level of impact in natural areas (0, 1, 3, 5, 10)   ____

                Total (50 possible)   ____

                A + B (100 possible)   ____

II. Feasibility of Control or Management

    A. Abundance Within Park

        1. Number of populations (1, 3, 5)   ____
        2. Areal extent of populations (1, 2, 3, 5)   ____

    B. Ease of Control

        1. Seed banks (0, 5, 15)   ____
        2. Vegetative regeneration (0, 5, 15)   ____
        3. Level of effort required (1, 5, 10, 15)   ____
        4. Abundance and proximity of propagules (0, 5, 10, 15)   ____

    C. Side Effects of Chemical/Mechanical Control (0, 5, 15)   ____

    D. Effectiveness of Community Management (0, 5, 10)   ____

    E. Biological Control (0, 5, 10)   ____

                                            Total (100 possible)   ____

Urgency: ____

Appendix C
Species Abstract of Canada Thistle
at Pipestone National Monument, Minnesota

Park: Pipestone National Monument

Species: *Cirsium arvense*
                                               (L.) Scop.

Common Name: Canada thistle, field thistle, creeping thistle, California
                                               thistle

Urgency Ranking: High

Overall Ranking: 8

Significance of Impact: 59
   A. Current impact: 19
   B. Ability to become a pest: 40

Feasibility of Control or Management: 17

Taxonomic Description:

Canada thistle is a dioecious, perennial forb reaching heights of up to 1.5 m. This species's erect stem
is highly branched above, green, and glabrescent-to-covered with dense cobweb-like hairs. Canada
thistle usually occurs in small to large patches with numerous individuals arising from horizontal, lateral
roots bearing adventitious shoots. Leaves are simple and placed alternately on the stem. Lower cauline
leaves are 5-18 cm long and 1.5-6 cm wide, oblong to oblanceolate, and entirely or shallowly to pinnately
lobed. Each lobe has few to many spines, and some spines are up to 5 mm in length. Both leaf
surfaces may be glabrous, or the upper surface may be lightly pubescent while the lower surface is
densely pubescent. Cauline leaves are reduced in size upwards and less lobed. Leaves may have a
petiole up to 1 cm long, sessile, clasping, or short decurrent. Heads are numerous and occur in
terminal corymb-like clusters. Each head is discoid and unisexual or incompletely dioecious. Pistillate
flowers are 1-2 cm high and 0.5-1 cm wide, and staminate flowers are somewhat shorter. Bracts are
imbricate, in five to six rows, ovate to lanceolate (2-6 mm long and up to 1.2 mm wide), spine-tipped
with a spine up to 1 mm long, and glabrous to covered with a dense cobweb-like hair. The corolla is
tubular and pink or purple in color (occasionally white). Staminate corolla tubes are 12-14 mm long,
and anthers are 3.5-4 mm long and occasionally have vestigial pistillate parts. Pistillate corollas are
longer (19-24 mm long) and may have vestigial anthers. Achenes are light brown to straw-colored (2-4
mm long and up to 1.5 mm wide). Each achene has a pappus of numerous white to grayish plumose
bristles reaching up to 2.5 cm in length. Four varieties of this species have been recognized: var.
vestitum Wimm. & Grab., var. *integrifolium* Wimm. & Grab., var. *arvense* (L.) Scop., and var. *horridum*
Wimm. & Grab.

Biology and Ecology:

Canada thistle is a highly competitive and noxious weed. It was apparently introduced from Eurasia into North America in colonial times as a contaminate of agricultural seed. Now a naturalized weed, Canada thistle is most commonly found in agricultural lands, pastures, and rangelands. The weed has also become established in forests, riversides, roadsides, lawns, gardens, abandoned fields, and ditchbanks. Canada thistle can now be found in all of the lower 48 states and all of the Canadian provinces.

Canada thistle is most common in open, mesophytic areas. It has a temperature tolerance of -35° to 40° C. Optimal annual precipitation is 400-750 mm. The species grows in a wide variety of soils, including sand dunes, but is most abundant in clayey soils. It can tolerate saline soils and wet or dry soils, but grows best in dry soils. Disturbance is necessary for initial establishment; however, once established it may rapidly spread by both rhizomes and seed. Canada thistle is not generally shade tolerant. Its growth is reduced when light falls to 60-70% of full daylight, and death occurs when light is reduced to 20% of full sun. This tolerance level may explain why Canada thistle does not persist in prairies in good to excellent condition. The species also does not readily tolerate waterlogged, poorly aerated soils. However, it may be found growing in these conditions in a lowered condition.

Extensive rhizomes of Canada thistle make it unique among the thistles. Rhizomes develop at depths far below the zone of rhizome development for most species. Most rhizome development occurs in the first 75 cm of the soil, but has been reported to occur at nearly 7 m. Lateral root growth of up to 6 m in one growing season has been recorded. Root buds are produced on lateral roots at 6-12-cm intervals. With these closely placed buds, root fragments as small as 8 mm in length and 3-6 mm thick have produced new shoots, and root fragments 13 cm in length nearly always produce new shoots. Root fragments can produce viable shoots in as few as five days. Root/shoot elongation increases with temperature and photoperiod. Elongation is greatest at 25°/15° C day/night temperatures, soil temperatures of 30° C, and a photoperiod of 15 hours. Root reserves are lowest just before flowering and are the greatest in early fall when aboveground growth stops.

Shoots begin to emerge in the early spring when soil temperatures reach about 5° C. Development of rosette leaves occurs first followed by vertical elongation in early summer. Flowering is generally from June to September, when day length reaches 14 to 18 hours. Canada thistle is incompletely dioecious, with the staminate and pistillate flowers usually borne on separate plants. Therefore, natural patches are usually of one sex. Flowers are pollinated by insects, primarily honey bees and some wasps. Each plant produces from 30 to 100 heads in a season. Each pistillate head has about 100 fertile florets, and about 83 to 90 will form seeds. One plant has the potential to produce up to 5,200 seeds in a season, but the average seed production is about 1,530 seeds per plant. Seeds are dispersed primarily by wind. Seed size is variable, averaging 650,000 to nearly 1,500,000 per kg.

Germination rates of between 50% and 95% have been observed. An average of 90% of the yearly seed production germinates within one year. Studies have shown that some seeds can remain viable in the soil for up to 21 years and up to four months in water. Optimal germination in the laboratory occurs with temperatures at a constant 30° C or where temperatures alternate between 20° and 30° C or 30° and 40° C. Germination is restricted with osmotic pressures above 5 bars. Optimal germination is between pH 5.8 and 7.0. Each crop of seed produces a succession of seedlings. Some will germinate that fall and produce a rosette. These will then flower the next summer. Other seeds will not germinate until the next spring (or later) and may or may not flower that year.

Some evidence indicates that Canada thistle may have an allelopathic effect; however, no specific compound has been isolated. Autotoxicity has been hypothesized in some circumstances.

Distribution:

An intermediate number of Canada thistle plants are present at Pipestone National Monument. They occur in patches and cover less than a total of 5 ha. Canada thistle plants are found in midsuccessional sites that were disturbed in the last 11 to 50 years. These plants have the potential to invade and modify existing native plant communities and may endanger the secondary successional resources. The plants have a minor visual impact on the park.

Control:

Numerous control options exist for Canada thistle. Biological, chemical, cultural, and mechanical methods have all been used with varying levels of success. An important consideration in controlling Canada thistle is that the seeds have the potential to remain viable in the seed bank for at least 20 years. Thus, removing living plants may not totally eliminate the problem. A further consideration is that many sources of new propagules surround the park.

An important consideration prior to applying any control method is to determine if enough desirable plants are present to replace the Canada thistle. If desirable vegetation is absent or not present in enough numbers, control will be of little value. Most control methods will have a detrimental effect on other plant species, and they all constitute a disturbance that will favor reinvasion by Canada thistle or by other exotic species. Researchers should note that many native thistles are present in the area, and they should not be subjected to control. Proper identification is important.

Frequent mowing over a number of years will control Canada thistle. Mowing has been the primary control method employed at Pipestone. Most studies indicate a need to mow patches of Canada thistle at least twice a year to prevent seed dispersal and reduce root reserves. Systematic monthly mowings may be necessary to prevent lateral flower bud development and to keep root reserves depleted. Tillage may be used to control Canada thistle; however, tillage may result in an increase in abundance due to spreading rootstalks and the subsequent disturbance. Tillage should be to a depth of 10 cm when the elongated shoots are 8 to 10 days old. Tillage should be repeated at a minimum of 21-day intervals. Canada thistle has a relatively high light requirement, and smother crops may provide some measure of control by shading. Smother plants that have been used include sweet clover, alfalfa, millet, sorghum, hemp, and small grains.

No prescribed burning studies have been conducted to specifically control Canada thistle. Supplementary information has shown that repeated burning in May or June reduced thistle abundance in grasslands. In most of these studies, Canada thistle showed an initial increase in abundance, followed by a notable reduction in abundance.

A number of chemical control options exist for Canada thistle. Many herbicides discussed here are not specific to Canada thistle or may not be specifically licensed for this particular type of use. Thus, users must read and follow all label directions. Before "modern" herbicides were introduced, compounds such as sodium chloride, sodium arsenite, calcium arsenite, sodium chlorate, and carbon bisulfide were all used in attempts to control Canada thistle. Numerous herbicides are now available for controlling Canada thistle. Tordon (picloram) is probably the most effective. Tordon may give a 95% control in the first year when applied at a rate of 0.56-1.23 kg ai/ha in the spring before flowering or in the fall during active rosette growth. Banvel (dicamba) applied at 0.56-6.73 kg ai/ha or 2,4-D (amine) at 0.56-2.24 kg ai/ha will suppress or control Canada thistle. However, more effective control may be achieved by combining the two herbicides in a 1:1 mixture. This mixture should be applied in the spring before flowering or in the fall when the rosettes are actively growing. Roundup (glyphosate) applied at a rate of 1-2 kg ai/ha at the bud stage or during the active growth period in the fall will also control this thistle. Amitrole-T (amitrol) applied at rates of 2.24-4.48 kg ai/ha when the plants are in the bud stage has yielded 70% control in the first year. Most herbicides, except Tordon, should not be applied while the plants are in a moisture-stressed condition. Other herbicides that have shown potential to control Canada thistle are Buctril 2EC (bromoxynil), Curtail (clopyralid plus 2,4-D), and Stinger (clopyralid).

Biological control of Canada thistle has received some attention. Over 80 native species of insects and over 50 species of animals and fungi use Canada thistle to some extent. A few species have the potential for providing some measure of control. Only four insects may be a threat to Canada thistle. These four are composed of two beetles [*Cassia rubiginosa* Muell. (Coleoptera: Chrysomelidae) and *Cleonus piger* (Coleoptera: Curculionidae)], one fly [*Orellia ruficauda* Fab. (Diptera: Tephritidae)], and the painted lady butterfly [*Vanessa cardui* L. (Lepidoptera: Nymphaidae)]. Only *Orellia ruficauda* appears to do significant damage to Canada thistle, and this level of damage is not sufficient for control. Five European insect species [*Ceutorhynchus litura* F. (Coleoptera: Curculionidae), *Rhinocyllus conicus* Froelich (Coleoptera: Curculionidae), *Altica carduorum* Guerin-Meneville (Coleoptera: Chrysomelidea), *Lema cyanella* L. (Coleoptera: Chrysomelidae), and *Urophora cardui* L. (Diptera: Tephritidae)] have all been released in North America for Canada thistle control. To date, only *Ceutorhynchus litura* has become established, spread, and begun to suppress this plant.

Fungus species of the genus *Puccinia* hold some promise as control agents. *Puccinia punctiformis* (Strauss) Roehling (Fungus: Uredinales) has been tested in Europe and New Zealand and has been found to only reduce plant vigor. The best biological control of Canada thistle has come when this fungus has been used in conjunction with either 2,4-D, or *Ceutorhynchus litura*. Plants treated with the fungus followed by weevil introduction had over a 50% increase in damage over nontreated plants.

References:

Evans, J.E. 1984. Canada thistle (*Cirsium arvense*): a literature review of management practices. Natural Areas Journal 4:11-21.

Forsyth, S.F. and A.K. Watson. 1985. Predispersal seed predation of Canada thistle. Canadian Entomologist 117:1075-1081.

Great Plains Flora Association. 1986. Flora of the Great Plains. University of Kansas Press, Lawrence. 1392 pp.

Haderlie, L.C., S. Dewey, and D. Kidder. 1987. Canada thistle biology and control. Bulletin 666. Cooperative Extension Service, University of Idaho, Moscow.

Haggar, R.J., A.K. Oswald, and W.G. Richardson. 1986. A review of the impact and control of creeping thistle (*Cirsium arvense* L.) in grassland. Crop Protection 5:73-76.

Higgins, R.E. and L.C. Erickson. 1960. Canada thistle identification and control. Bulletin 338. Cooperative Extension Service, University of Idaho, Moscow.

Hodgson, J.M. 1968. The nature, ecology and control of Canada thistle. Technical Bulletin 1386. U.S. Department of Agriculture.

Julian, M.H., editor. 1987. Biological control of weeds. CAB International, Wallingford, Oxon, United Kingdom.

Knake, E.L., L. Wrage, D. Childs, B. Majek, C. Bryson, and J. Hull, editors. 1991. Weed Control Manual. Meister Publishing Company, Willoughby, Ohio. 410 pp.

Lorenzi, H.J. and L.S. Jeffery. 1987. Weeds of the United States and Their Control. Van Nostrand Reinhold Company Incorporated, New York. 355 pp.

Magnusson, M.U., D.L. Wyse, and J.M. Spitzmueller. 1987. Canada thistle (*Cirsium arvense*) propagation from stem sections. Weed Science 35:637-639.

Moore, R.J. 1975. The biology of Canadian weeds. 13. *Cirsium arvense* (L.) Scop. Canadian Journal of Plant Science 55:1033-1048.

Nebraska Cooperative Extension Service. 1991. A 1991 guide for herbicide use in Nebraska. EC 91-130. University of Nebraska, Lincoln.

Radosevich, S.R. and J. S. Holt. 1984. Weed Ecology Implications for Vegetation Management. John Wiley & Sons, New York. 265 pp.

Sather, N. 1988. Element Stewardship Abstract for *Cirsium arvense* - Canada Thistle. The Nature Conservancy, Minneapolis.

Wilson. R.G. and L.C. Haderlie. 1980. Canada thistle. G80-509. Nebraska Cooperative Extension Service, University of Nebraska, Lincoln.

Whitson, T.D., editor. 1987. Weeds and poisonous plants of Wyoming and Utah. Cooperative Extension Service, University of Wyoming, Laramie, Cooperative Extension Service and Agricultural Experiment Station, Utah State University, Logan. 281 pp.

Local Control Experts:

Extension Weed Specialist
Department of Agronomy and Plant Genetics
University of Minnesota
St. Paul, MN 55155
(612) 625-5753

Department of Natural Resources
Box 25 DNR Building
500 Lafayette Rd.
St. Paul, MN 55155
(612) 296-0778

Notes